CONTENT KINGS

CONTENT KINGS

Crafting Winning Strategies for Digital Domination

FIONA STERLING

QuantumQuill Press

CONTENTS

CHAPTER 1

Introduction

We study the responses of brands attempting to transition to new digital channels in a publishing world offering soft news - Information Entertainment (IE) - hard news. Many content-producing sectors experience a tension between commons content increasing large-market publishers' advertising revenues, and fiscal pressures lessening their ability to produce time-consuming, quality information. Given the sink-or-swim nature of online advertising revenue, can an undisclosed winner emerge? We use the Spotify Engineering Culture platform as work in the software company most responsive to consumer attention historic Zen optimum, to identify best practice for digital newcomers. We then apply this insight to vulnerable incumbents.

The publishing world faces ongoing transformative change driven by digital - rapid growth in time and money spent online, and social networks' and search engines' command of user attention and website traffic. History suggests smaller brands should rapidly become winners and losers. Strong brands P&G and prominent bricks-and-mortar (B&M) retailers Tesco and Walmart rule the retail world; the retail battlefield is littered with the corpses of once-famous entities. Fast-moving consumer goods (FMCG) firms have disrupted traditional supermarkets by selling directly to consumers online. Newspaper and music publishers have seen strong brands shift part of their content sales revenues to new channels controlled by others. Should incumbents launch full-scale defence to prevent business degradation, attack non-traditional players with a radical new digital offering, or collaborate with other traditional publishers in response?

CHAPTER 2

Understanding the Digital Landscape

Other research topics related to this research were privacy, open data, digital ad-block, sentiment analysis, and wearable devices. The policies in the digital environment will affect not only privacy but also open data sharing, data secondary usage, and a data dump leading to increasingly opaque media as well as the environment for sentiment analysis and wearable devices. That is, if surveillance activity is not properly managed, the effort to reconstruct the surveillance market and the desire of the digital environment policy will conflict with each other. Hence, this study aims to examine the consequences of unmanaged surveillance activities in today's digital market and to lay a foundation for the establishment of public policy on surveillance. A second goal is to understand which data can actually be collected from the behavior model of a specific user, to estimate the reliability of user behavior prediction and the prediction accuracy of user behavior in a panoptic digital world, and to quantize privacy in the digital panoptic world.

To better understand the digital universe, information seeking behavior should be analyzed using the concept of surveillance. Surveillance was first studied based on institutions and targets, and the criticisms of this approach were proposed in the electronic panopticon system. However, the relation between surveillance and advertising was rarely considered, so relevant studies were limited. Therefore, the surveillant marketing concept has been suggested, in which marketing and surveillance are closely related, and marketing activities are understood and understood through the process of data flow. However, there is still a lack of study on how the "dump of the data" exchanged in the market is combined and used for advertising targeting, as well as on changes in the social environment, the behavioral structure of the users, and privacy. Also, privacy protection is becoming more important with the rapid growth of the surveillance market.

According to the International Data Corporation (IDC), the digital universe will nearly double in size every two years. Companies will not be able to keep up with this relentless pace, and as such, companies with the capabilities to comprehend the digital media world, harness the data and intelligence, and create market-winning strategies will be at the forefront of the digital market. Knowledge about people, business, media, and society, science, engineering, and computing, and smart planet (Figure 20.1) is vital to comprehend the digital landscape effectively.

CHAPTER 3

Identifying Target Audiences

Barrels of ink have been used to decry how misinformation, disinformation and propaganda find their way to the top of the virtual stacks of information competing for consumer eyeballs. So how do you avoid the fake news and get to the consumers? It is crucial to understand the various types of searches people conduct. They often fall into three categories: general information interest (learn something), navigate (location-based inquiry) or purchase (justification or affirmation of decision). Based on a research program developed by a trainer at Google, PR clients and organizations need to know what their targets can be attracted by.

Just as with traditional media, PR and marketing communications professionals planning online activities for their clients or organizations need to identify target audiences. Doing so, however, entails a great deal more than simply dividing the market up by age, gender, geography, interests, and purchase history. Online communicators need to understand what the members of their target audiences do in the digital space. Based on all of this information, articulating syndication strategies for getting stories placed in the content streams of the identified personalities is necessary. By allowing the appropriate online personalities to tell stories when and if they are ready, Google algorithms and the consumers that utilize search will perpetuate these stories by shining the spotlight on them.

CHAPTER 4

Creating Compelling Content

Custom high-resolution images demonstrate commitment to your publication and are a magnificent compliment to your writings. Images speak louder than words at times, and never lose importance with time. Not only are images a lovely addition to each story, but they complement and add value to your content. It is essential to get close to and understand one's community to produce content that is truly relevant. Millennial readers are smarter than any generation before when it comes to filtering out the hype. Their digital fluency allows them to identify "shill" content in a matter of seconds. Communities must be treated with the utmost respect, and not be taken for granted. Many publishers have attempted to extend old narratives through to the digital medium. Readers regularly reject such efforts when they perceive that these narratives are lacking in relevance.

The best content has these seven qualities: 1) It is original, 2) It tells a complete story, 3) It has high production values, 4) It comes from a writer with knowledge of the subject, 5) It has unique images, 6) It speaks to, and comes from, a community of mission-centric readers and 7) It doesn't exist mere for the sake of extending a narrative at the cost of relevance. Original content is authentic and creates a meaningful connection between the writer and the reader. A reader will only engage with your content if it tells a complete story that is clear, concise, and human-focused. High production values are proof of respect for your readers, and contribute to the retention of new readers. Who has more authority on a subject than the writer or the reader of a publication? The reader is the student, the mentor, and the expert.

CHAPTER 5

Leveraging Social Media Platforms

It's not uncommon at all for a company to combine paid and organic social, and that's a great combination. Your organic media forms the credibility for your inbound, is the conduit to authoritative ranking that drives SEO, and the first pass at DISQUS / Livefyre for a place like Reddit, so it's part of a healthy marketing strategy. But it's not sufficient for getting into the feed for the people you really need to be posting in the feed of. So it's good to be aware that your next step into social is going to have to look more like an ad spend than your favorite inbound channel. One important item still remains prevalent with each success story of content kings — a strong public relations approach. It is often the case (but not always) that the press agitates the water, the brand dips its toes in, its agencies take note and pull together a marketing / content strategy, which is then holistically influenced, along with the press, as one moves into unison with the other.

For the fastest and simplest initial dissemination of your content, think in terms of leveraging social media platforms, but keep up with the rapidly evolving rules, regulations, and requirements for leveraging paid or organic social. Social technologies have gone from being "mildly interesting" to being worth $100 billion dollars, and the road has been paved with failure after expensive failure of companies trying to "buy, own and control" the user base of one of the industry incumbents: Facebook, Twitter, and LinkedIn. So it will only make sense for some evolution to be happening in this area, and soon. But if I were that person, where structurally I'd be in charge, I would like to take my chances in the area which is ripe for some disruption, which you are already seeing through the kind of start-ups in 2013 doing social specifically for the enterprises. This is an evolution of a different kind – an evolution that is a throwback to pre- or at least predominantly-individual-social, i.e. it's email all over again.

CHAPTER 6

Search Engine Optimization (SEO) Techniques

This study will not delve into advanced SEO babbles which might involve microdata, structured data, image optimization, thin content, onsite ranking factors, and other concepts that only website developers might understand. The paper will concern itself with search engines' jump-through-hoops techniques that ordinary people and small businesses might apply. To learn about advanced SEO, one should follow and learn from websites that teach proper application of 2016 and 2017 SEO. It is about adding user satisfaction to SEO techniques. The new paradigm of use in ranking is that webpages should show proof of usefulness – evidence of user satisfaction in advancing to the searchers. One could understand what audience want by using Google Analytics platform to track website metrics such as conversions, bounces, time on site, page views, user demographics, traffic sources, etc. These metrics are called Key Performance Indicators (KPIs) or vanity metrics. Google provides reliable up-to-the-minute tutorials and educational contents about their search ranking algorithms. One could also use these free contents to fine-tune its website ranking in Google and other search engines. When website creators create satisfying contents for audience, Google's search engine results page (SERP) ranking will rise.

Arguments abound on what search engine optimization (SEO) is and what attaining high ranks on search engine results pages means to businesses. Many people believe that it is a pure copywriting mechanism, while others believe that SEO is purely about algorithmic adjustments to a webpage. Both views are erroneous. SEO has two basic dimensions – pure copywriting techniques that are used in crafting contents for a website and other methods employed in increasing search ranking. One thing is certain, without decent copies, high ranking would produce high bounce rate. This makes content creation a necessary skill in successful SEO; and where there is reliance on competitive advantage; electronic commerce.

CHAPTER 7

Building an Engaged Community

More significantly, proper SEO-literate business-dedicated sites can be expected to possess the vast skills and experiences necessary to add generators for if not new ideas, calls for action to subscribe, and general questions – or at least to provide educative responses. Furthermore, those same sites are more ideally placed to take full advantage of the potential that the Fourth Generation is currently and will in the future offer to websites. Just a few of the examples provided by the author also highlight websites that have the ability to rank well in the general search engines.

Indeed, many companies have seen resounding success thanks to social media (for example, Facebook, Twitter, LinkedIn). For the most part, successful social media sites have compelled internet users to register with their site – and not have to pay to register – so that following their registration they become repeat visitors/subscribers, participating in discussions, polls/surveys, and questions/responses, as well as creating content (for example, submitting links, uploading videos, and listing related news). It's one of the author's positions that the central task here is "topic development" (a purposive history study on this subject, in this unique context). Additionally, these types of sites generally have their pages designed to load fast. Consequently, it should be emphasized that a large percentage of the success of these social media sites is due to their focus on providing opportunities for their subscribers to quickly publish relativistic thoughts to existing ideas (in other words, for the Shifting-the-Focus craze). This is something with which no business site necessarily aspires, let alone concludes that they are successfully applying.

So, how can businesses maintain the attention of so-called qualified people on their site and ultimately get that sought-after word-of-mouth marketing? First off, it has to be acknowledged that not all successful online business sites are chock full of management articles (a typical term applied by the author to short page content on SEO-literate business-dedicated sites, with the concept cut out to include other readers).

Once you have your website established, you might think that all the hard work has been done. After all, you've written the content and designed something that exemplifies your thought leadership or improved your search rankings, right? Wrong! Experienced CEOs, webmasters, and SEO practitioners all understand that it is not just inbound links that boost rankings. Now that we've attracted visitors and we've moved up in ranking, we need people who visit our site to stay there and for them to tell others how great it was. Unfortunately, they don't always do that, particularly for short page content (except social media content), which is mainly what persists at least in the present and potentially the future, regardless of the possible amendments to search engine algorithms and rating signals.

CHAPTER 8

Harnessing the Power of Influencers

In settings like India, where poor infrastructure can pose a burden on small businesses, large companies tend to struggle with issues offered to them due to the nature of their size, coordinating their management, and their often-defined operations. The main scientific principle we wish to portray is a desk review that linearly provides implementation guidelines according to the viable tactics for the goals corporations seek to reach in partnering with influencers, combining and finally implementing in a way that was best appropriate for companies operating in a complicating regional technological and political landscapes like India. Oosterveer believes that companies are more and more unaware that they still operate at the pace of the 1910s.

Influencer marketing is currently one of the most effective strategies for selling a brand to customers in competitive social landscapes. Yet, a reasonable strategy has not been provided for large companies in general guidance. Our practical analysis concerning multinational companies in India found, in general, that because of the increasing polemics of the strong influence in attractive applications of data science, a combination of managerial flexibility could be the solution. Companies are generally falling short of their developing corporate strategies through harnessing the power of young, naturally impressive strategic public relations skills, and the micro outreach of influencers. While they continue to grow increasingly internet-ready and prolific, the companies oftentimes approach the internet the same way that the manufacturers operated in the first years of automation.

CHAPTER 9

Monetizing Content

A few of the tried and true ways of monetizing content are the benefits of freemium model, where users are able to use some portion of services or products at no charge. Open source software, platforms, and video hosting does require some sort of investment to create the physical product. Many times one can just create a small content teaser and see what type of responses it gets before making big decisions. Ad-supported platforms are usually very easily sold and tend to generate a consistent type of revenue. This type of plan monetizes the actual usage of a service. Paid-for content normally requires an audience to already be established. Advertising has the highest rate in search, then email, then text, but they all are somewhere between 1.5-6 in the range of ROI.

One of the challenges in content creation is to figure out how and with what to monetize that will keep you in business and on schedule with creating it. Figuring out content creation was a major step. Now that you have identified and started creating the content you are going to use, there are many ways to monetize it. Generally, businesses should use participatory forms, such as polls and quizzes. Action and special offer forms can be used to generate revenue and typically look to do better than the participatory ones, but typically have a lower conversion rate. "The nine questions regarding content monetization... who pays, what content strategy is being fulfilled, what are we trying to achieve, is it going to position us ahead of the competition and what action are we trying to achieve, while not devaluing the brand, and what are the indirect effects to watch for? Will it help with branding and marketing? Will it help with customer service?"

CHAPTER 10

Analyzing and Measuring Success

The different metrics I've listed are a mix of long-term business metrics and shorter-term indicators of content success. Other long-term business-wide metrics include: "Gross margin," "Cost per acquisition," "Return visits," "Outbound links," and "Shares per visits." To work with these, you'll need to use web analytics tools, as well as platforms that can create dashboards. There's an overwhelming number of tools available for both web analytics and the visualization of these metrics. Here are some tools that we have used or know people who have found these valuable. In March 2016, Google launched its free data visualization tool Data Studio. Data Studio lets you import your website data and create reports to visualize your numbers. It is quick to set up, intuitive to use, and you can easily share your reports with other people, which makes it the most user-friendly enterprise-level reporting tool as of March 2016.

In every chapter, we have broken down key aspects of being a successful content king. However, we haven't yet discussed how you can analyze and measure your success. Early on, when you're designing your strategy, you will need to define measures in order to monitor your progress. Once you're in full flight, you will need to keep iterating and innovating to stay relevant. Success means different things to different businesses. However, many of the metrics you might use have overall goals for the business. For example, if your goal is to grow traffic to your site, you might track individual campaigns and see the traffic they generate. Whatever metrics you use, you need to keep measuring and analyzing these numbers. They will tell you whether you need to make tweaks to your strategy. By tracking metrics and pushing them into dashboards, you can keep everyone in your business aware of our progress. You can also use them to make better-informed decisions.

CHAPTER 11

Staying Ahead of Trends

To stay ahead of trends, marketers must continuously invest in learning and improvement. Attend major expert-led events. Review the best blogs of European experts in addition to globally known advisors. However, the biggest time and resources investment has to be allocated to early stage, product-focused testing of best-in-class ideas. Don't fall behind. As an increasing amount of businesses answer your successes with full resources—and anticipation past the exhaustion of digital—which might still be young in a day or in decades past, be ready and take courage. A best-in-class laboratory of London, Paris, Berlin or settling right in a small home in Innamonth can help you invest wisely.

Content kings staying ahead of trends. In our hyper competitive, $1 billion plus digital marketing industry, with thousands of businesses presenting at dozens of events every day, it is absolutely essential to stay one to ten steps ahead. As accelerating factors, such as digital micro revolutions, lessons from a previous platform (what can Facebook marketers learn even before launching ad campaigns from Instagram!), and successful case studies burst forth, this task becomes increasingly difficult. Nevertheless, major trends are an essential aspect of digital domination and a crucial part of a content leader's strategy—dominate a new channel or discipline before most get there.

CHAPTER 12

Scaling Your Digital Presence

Following are areas to take into heavy consideration when planning and building on our digital platforms. This should not be taken as a comprehensive list of bullet points as I decided to go into detail with some answers I felt that I have gotten access to somewhat formed by seeing some pretty nice results from application. Each business is unique, and each offers uniqueness to the client or customer, so some factors important to it are not so important to others. With that disclaimed, here are a few serious areas to watch (in no particular order) when scaling your digital presence to competitive levels.

The only question is how to scale? What are the things that we need to ensure are done right and learned from? Remember, any of us who make a living by providing digital or digitalized goods and services are up against the biggest centralized source of information on earth, which also happens to be competitive on the open market. What we are offering may be different or similar, but what we have to do when it comes to dominating in the digital space is very much the same.

Pretty much everything is on about scaling these days - and for good reason, as our world is evolving faster than the human consciousness can keep up with. There are very few industries where you can relax with processes and strategies from the past and expect to thrive for a long time (those running funeral homes are sitting quite pretty, but even they have to scale). Digital is very much the kind of the information age (I believe that even our very detailed descriptions in the last chapter were put together in a matter of days due to the nature of digital existence).

CHAPTER 13

Protecting and Managing Your Online Reputation

There is much more content to be created than published online, according to the idiom "the tip of the iceberg." Increasing that tip's depth is the secret formula of digital content domination. Companies who craft and produce their own content diminish the visibility of unwelcome third-party content. To protect your brand's reputation and rightfully stand in the digital spotlight, your company must produce all of its digital content. Companies must sign and have all employees sign employment contracts that include non-compete and intellectual property clauses to retrieve the content souvenirs employees "take home" when they leave the company.

It is easier than ever for your online reputation to be tarnished. Words travel fast, and content shows up on Google searches within minutes. In just one minute, Facebook users share almost 2.5 million pieces of content, Twitter users tweet almost 300,000 times, YouTube users upload 72 hours of video, and Instagram users post nearly 220,000 new photos. You must respond quickly and with your best communication position whenever criticisms of your business get published.

CHAPTER 14

Collaborating with Other Content Creators

Search for the households/brands you are liking. The idea is to expand your net to perhaps identify those people who were not looking at the "Having Fun with the Kids" household. Stop assuming that just because they are not running their YouTube channels as you do, they would not have suggestions that are pertinent to you. The quest is to find collaborators or masterminds who do not possess pressing hangouts to entertain, do celebrity hauls, or premium "No Thumbnail" vlogs. Meet up with them. Director and camera capabilities, stylized filming and styling skills, tagging and SEO theories. There is an array of potentially collaborative learning opportunities from people who are not directly doing exactly what you are doing.

After identifying possible candidates who will be happy to have you on their projects, start your outreach with a small collaboration – comments on their existing video, then on their social media. Link one or two content pieces. After building interest, suggest a small collaboration to see how well your creativity will vibe with theirs.

Should it be a total smash, other creators will host you in their most-viewed video category – the kind of social proof that will take your numbers to a whole new level.

Collaboration can significantly expand your reach and breathe new energy into your own content creation. For successful collaborations, give before you expect to receive. As small as it may seem, constructive comments on other YouTubers' work can mean the world, especially for smaller creators. The idea is to engage with people who may not be directly competing with your content but would be happy to introduce you to their own subscriber base. It is easier for a hairdresser to collaborate with an Aromatherapy expert on an advanced hairstyle. Less competition, shared expertise. The same applies to digital content creators.

CHAPTER 15

Expanding to New Platforms and Formats

The digital marketing efforts of any brand will prosper if the creators of the content are supplied with an array of formats. We have dozens of profiles that need their biographies updated for very similar purposes, but their applications and situations are unique, which is why we have encountered a workflow driven by decision trees. Also, do not assume the strategy should be the same for every new form you intend to publish. Customize your copy, the structure, tone, and network you utilize. The audience you want to reach influences these choices, the expectations, opportunities, chances to attract, any goals, and the risks. An analysis of what messages should be interchanged can be conducted to discover the identity of the audience. Digital marketers have developed the approaches included in this tool of analyzing data to guarantee that the interpretation begins to correspond to the anticipated outcomes of the audience. Development of flexible and dynamic content is only possible when a vehicle of influence seeks to create an influence.

Maestros of digital content creation, the Content Kings consistently succeed in creating copy that outshines the competition. Case in point, our influencer campaign work attracts 2.8 billion social media impressions yearly. Excellent in strategy, the Kings bring to bear processes that transform complex information into pieces intended to give audiences a clear understanding of the client's unique value proposition. With years of experience, the Content Kings are flexible in accommodating the change in brand and industry measures and are able to achieve an acceleration in agency productivity and effectiveness.

CHAPTER 16

Embracing Innovation in the Digital Space

News publications are not the only ones that are experimenting with AI. The resulting hype around it and the very real promise of improved productivity and risk analysis caused some investment banks to pass on habitually insular R&D and let the inner - and in some rare cases, collaborative - geek out. Perhaps smaller companies are even better suited for upbeat heads-experimentation dance. When software-as-a-service company OutSystems decided to help digital marketing company AdRoll optimize the process of analyzing, organizing and leveraging its customer data, employees from teams across AdRoll were taught the basics of data science through a six-week course. At the end, the trained 'citizen data scientists' were able to submit their data science projects for a chance to win a monetary prize. In a much bigger attempt at the democratization of big data, the European Union is set to create a pool of more than two thousand researchers and enrollment, and possible paid training, in a comprehensive data science bootcamp.

Sometimes, even the best content will grow stale. Still, there is no room for panic - with the speed of digital, your homage to yesterday may soon become today's dark horse or even the inspiration for your competitor's next big thing. A prime example of a once-solid project with an uncertain future is Reuters.com. Well aware of the trend of paid mobile news, the agency now charges for access to text news on all platforms. Back in 2017, the company's Eikon customers got access to the bot that turned Reuters news into human-like speech. The bot can scan the market information and crunch it to provide the user with a condensed round-up of the news.